ephesians

Living in God's Family

Neighborhood Bible Studies Publishers
Dobbs Ferry, New York

Living in God's Family

12 Discussions for Group Bible Study
Marilyn Kunz and Catherine Schell

Scripture quotations, unless otherwise indicated, are taken from the HOLY BIBLE, NEW INTERNATIONAL VERSION®. Copyright © 1973, 1978, 1984 by International Bible Society. Used by permission of Zondervan Publishing House. All rights reserved.

All rights reserved. No part of this book may be reproduced or transmitted in any form or by any means, electronic or mechanical, including photocopying, recording, or any information storage and retrieval system without written permission from Neighborhood Bible Studies, 34 Main Street, Dobbs Ferry, New York, 10522.

Copyright © 1965 by Neighborhood Bible Studies as *Ephesians and Philemon*.

Revised 1996.

Copyright © 1996 by Neighborhood Bible Studies.
ISBN 1-880266-23-7
Printed in the United States of America
Cover by Tom Greene

CONTENTS

How to Use This Discussion Guide 7

Introduction to the Letter to the Ephesians 11

Discussion 1   **Acts 18—20; Ephesians 1—6**
Getting the Big Picture 13

Discussion 2   **Ephesians 1:1-14**
The Purpose of God 17

Discussion 3   **Ephesians 1:15-23**
That You Might Know Him Better 21

Discussion 4   **Ephesians 2:1-10**
Alive in Christ 25

Discussion 5   **Ephesians 2:11-22**
God's New Society 29

Discussion 6   **Ephesians 3:1-13**
Sent to the Gentiles 33

Discussion 7   **Ephesians 3:14-21**
For This Reason I Kneel 37

Discussion 8   **Ephesians 4:1-16**
We Belong to One Another 41

Discussion 9   **Ephesians 4:17-32**
New Clothes to Wear 45

Discussion 10   **Ephesians 5:1-20**
Light and Darkness 49

Discussion 11   **Ephesians 5:21—6:9**
New Relationships 53

Discussion 12   **Ephesians 6:10-24**
Stand Firm 57

What Should Our Group Study Next? 61

Ephesians

HOW TO USE THIS DISCUSSION GUIDE

This study guide uses the inductive approach to Bible study. *It will help you discover for yourself what the Bible says.* It will not give you prepackaged answers. *People remember most what they discover for themselves and what they express in their own words.* The study guide provides three kinds of questions:

1. What does the passage say? What are the facts?

2. What is the meaning of these facts?

3. How does this passage apply to your life?

Observe the facts carefully before you interpret the meaning of your observations. Then apply the truths you have discovered to life today. Resist the temptation to skip the fact questions since we are not as observant as we think. Find the facts quickly so you can spend more time on their meaning and application.

The purpose of Bible study is not just to know more Bible truths, but to apply them. Allow these truths to make a difference in how you think and act, in your attitudes and relationships, in the quality and direction of your life.

Each discussion requires about one hour. Decide on the amount of time to add for socializing and prayer.

Share the leadership. If a different person is the moderator or question-asker each week, interest grows and members feel the group belongs to everyone. The Bible is the authority in the group, not the question-asker.

When a group grows to more than ten, the quiet people become quieter. Plan to grow and multiply. You can meet as two groups in the same house or begin another group so that more people can participate and benefit.

Tools For An Effective Bible Study

1. A study guide for each person in the group.

2. A modern translation of the Bible such as:
    New International Version (NIV)
    Good News Bible (GNB)
    Jerusalem Bible (JB)
    New American Standard Bible (NASB)
    New English Bible (NEB)
    Revised Standard Version (RSV)

3. An English dictionary.

4. A map of the Lands of the Bible in a Bible or in this study guide.

5. Your conviction that the Bible is worth studying.

Guidelines For Effective Study

1. Stick to the passage under discussion.

2. Avoid tangents. If the subject is not addressed in the passage, put it on hold until after the study.

3. Let the Bible speak for itself. Do not quote other authorities or rewrite it to say what you want it to say.

4. Apply the passage personally and honestly.

5. Listen to one another to sharpen your insights.

6. Prepare by reading the Bible passage and thinking through the questions during the week.

7. Begin and end on time.

Helps For The Question-Asker

1. Prepare by reading the passage several times, using different translations if possible. Ask for God's help in understanding it. Consider how the questions might be answered. Observe which questions can be answered quickly and which may require more time.

2. Begin on time.

3. Lead the group in opening prayer or ask someone ahead of time to do so. Don't take anyone by surprise.

4. Ask for a different volunteer to read each Bible section. Read the question. Wait for an answer. Rephrase the question if necessary. Skip questions already answered by the discussion. Resist the temptation to answer the question yourself.

5. Encourage everyone to participate. Ask the group, "What do the rest of you think?" "What else could be added?"

6. Receive all answers warmly. If needed, ask, "In which verse did you find that?" "How does that fit with verse...?"

7. If a tangent arises, ask, "Do we find the answer to that here?" Or suggest, "Let's write that down and look for the information as we go along."

8. Discourage members who are too talkative by saying, "When I read the next question, let's hear from someone who hasn't spoken yet today."

9. Use the summary questions to bring the study to a conclusion on time.

10. Close the study with prayer.

11. Decide on one person to be the host and another person to be the question-asker for the next discussion.

INTRODUCTION to the Letter to the EPHESIANS

Paul's ministry in Ephesus began in earnest on his third missionary journey when he stayed more than two years teaching and preaching. As was his custom, he began his outreach with the Jews, but when opposition to the message was obvious, he moved into the lecture hall of Tyrannus. During that time we are told that all the residents of the province of Asia heard the word of the Lord.

Ephesus, strategically located on the crossroads between east and west, was surrounded by 230 independent communities within the Roman province of Asia. Thus the impact of Paul's mission went far beyond the city of Ephesus itself. Those who came to the city on business could not fail to hear of what was happening. They took the message back home where new groups of believers were established. It is probable that this letter was a circular intended for Gentile converts throughout Asia Minor.

The letter is a marvelous summary of the Good News. Many believe it is the crown of Paul's writings because it is concise, comprehensive and contemporary. It was not written to combat any error but simply to contemplate the implications of God's overall plan for his church and the world. It is breathtaking in its scope. Yet Paul's purpose is not merely to inspire. He relates these grand truths to the practical demands of Christian living in a hostile society.

About A.D. 62, Paul wrote this letter from Rome where he was under house arrest. His friends were free to visit him, and he sent this letter with Tychicus, a native of Ephesus, who was returning to Asia Minor. Perhaps because the letter may have been intended as a circular, Paul does not deal with particular issues but with the grandeur of the gospel and the lifestyle of those who believe.

Biblical scholar John R.W. Stott writes of this book, "God's new society—the church—is characterized by life in place of death, by unity and reconciliation in place of division and alienation, by the wholesome standards of righteousness in place of the corruption of wickedness, by love and peace in place of hatred and strife, and by unremitting conflict with evil in place of flabby confrontation with it. This vision of a new community has stirred me deeply."*

---

* John R.W. Stott, *God's New Society, The Message of Ephesians* (England: InterVarsity Press, 1979), 9-10.

DISCUSSION 1

Getting the Big Picture

Acts 18—20; Ephesians 1—6

Advance preparation:

Who were these Ephesians? How did they become Christians? As preparation for the study of this letter, read Acts 18—20 to learn how the gospel came to Ephesus and nearby cities of Asia Minor.

Then read through the letter Paul wrote to the Ephesians. Picture yourself as a member of the group of believers in Ephesus, eager to know what Paul had written. Everyone would want to hear the whole letter, not just part of it. Read it as eagerly as they did to get an overview of what Paul is writing about, without getting bogged down with details. (The original letter did not have chapters and verses to divide its thoughts.)

When you meet for your first study, use these discussion questions for a group overview of the letter.

Read Ephesians 1—6

1. Using a modern paragraphed translation, ask one person to go through the whole letter reading aloud only the first verse or complete sentence of each paragraph. Other group members should listen

rather than following in their Bibles. This exercise will remind you of the main ideas of the letter.

2. What thoughts or ideas impress you from reading this letter?

   Why does Paul write it?

3. How does the first half of the letter (chapters 1—3) differ from the second half (chapters 4—6)?

   Why is this order important?

4. If this were your only source of information about Paul, what would you know about him, his job, his situation, his ambitions, etc.? See 1:1, 16; 3:1-4, 7-9, 13; 4:1; 6:19, 20.

5. From your survey of this letter, what do you learn about the people to whom the letter is written?

6. Using information from Acts 18—20, what do you learn about the society in which these Christians live?

7. Imagine yourself as a first-century resident of Asia Minor who hears the reading of this letter. What impression would you have of Jesus Christ and of what it means to be his follower?

Summary

The believers in Ephesus have radically changed lives because of their commitment to Jesus Christ as Lord and Savior. Paul writes this letter to help them understand the scope and purpose of what God is doing in the world. God is creating a new family, a new society of which they are part—a people who are in sharp contrast to the world around them. The church as a body and its individual members are to *be for the praise of his glory* (1:12). This letter gives the practical teaching about how this should work out in the everyday lives of Christians.

Prayer

Heavenly Father, we eagerly await your teaching as we study this letter together. Thank you that you have an eternal purpose for our lives that goes beyond what we can see. We want to listen to your teaching with genuine humility, realizing afresh what a wonderful salvation you have given us in Christ Jesus, our Lord. Help us to live this week in light of your great purpose in saving us. For Jesus' sake. Amen.

Ephesians

Discussion 2

The Purpose of God

Ephesians 1:1-14

What is life for? Everyone needs a purpose for living, a meaning for existence. In this study, Paul spells out God's cosmic plan that takes believers beyond themselves into the mystery of God's purpose in Christ. He begins this letter with a salutation (verses 1, 2) followed by a thanksgiving (verses 3-14). Paul's thanksgiving is extensive, explaining the wonder of God's plan for us—a plan that stretches and enlarges our concepts of what it means to be a Christian.

Read Ephesians 1:1, 2

1. How does Paul describe himself and the source of his authority?

   Read Acts 22:6-16 to hear in his own words how Paul came to be an apostle, "one who is sent with a message."

2. Paul describes the Christians to whom he is writing as *the saints* and *the faithful.* From the context and using a dictionary, how would you define these words?

3. Paul says that these believers have two homes: in Ephesus and in Christ. What is the significance of being in both places for these believers, and for you as you substitute the name of your city in place of Ephesus?

*Note: To be **in Christ** is to be personally and vitally united to Christ, as branches are to a vine. To be a Christian is to be **in Christ**.*

4. Paul combines the Greek **grace** and the Hebrew **peace** in his greeting. What does each mean?

   Who is the source of both?

*Note: **Grace** and **peace** are key words throughout this letter. Be on the lookout for further references to these themes.*

Read Ephesians 1:3-14

5. List briefly everything God has done for the Christian in verses 3-14.

6. Look for all the times Paul uses the phrase **in Christ** or similar phrases. Why is this significant?

7. According to verses 4 and 5, what choice did God make?

   When and for what purpose did he make it (verses 4, 6, 12, 14)?

8. In practical terms for daily living, what does it mean to you to live **for the praise of his glory?**

9. What has it cost God to give the gifts mentioned in verses 7 and 8?

10. What do redemption and forgiveness mean for the person who receives them?

Read verses 7 and 8 in J.B. Phillips' translation, or Good News Bible.

11. What is the *mystery* that God has made known?

*Note: **Mystery** in the New Testament means something undiscoverable by human reason which must be revealed by God.*

12. How is God's power over time and over the universe described in verses 9-11?

13. How does God's purpose for the Christian affect the way you live your daily life (verse 12)?

14. What does it mean to you to be *marked with a seal, the promised Holy Spirit* (verses 13, 14; Acts 2:38)?

Note: A seal is a mark of ownership, a stamp of authenticity.

15. What does it mean that the Holy Spirit is the *deposit* guaranteeing your inheritance?

    Compare with 1 Peter 1:3-5.

16. What do the terms *truth* and *gospel* in verse 13 tell about the Christian message?

    When did you hear the gospel and know it was the truth?

*Note: The common hope of Jews and Gentiles is introduced in verses 12 and 13. **The first to hope in Christ** were of Jewish background, but **you also were included** is written to*

Gentile believers. Paul will develop this theme further in chapter 2.

Summary

1. What have you learned about the meaning of life for the believer *in Christ* ?

2. How is God—Father, Son and Holy Spirit—involved in your salvation?

Prayer

Praise be to the God and Father of our Lord Jesus Christ. You have blessed us with every spiritual blessing beyond what we can understand or have yet experienced. Thank you for making us your children. Thank you for the death of Christ which freed us from sin's penalty, and for the Holy Spirit who lives in us, assuring us of our hope of heaven. Help us to be glad about these glorious truths throughout the week, and to speak often to others about the wonder of your grace. For the praise of your glory. Amen.

DISCUSSION 3

That You Might Know Him Better

Ephesians 1:15-23

Paul extols God for his incredible gifts to us in Christ Jesus in the first half of chapter one. He begins his letter by blessing God for having blessed us in Christ Jesus. Now in the last half of the chapter he prays that God will open our eyes and our experience to the fullness of that blessing. Paul gives us a model for prayer not only in his persistence—*I keep asking*—but also in a good balance between praise to God for his blessings and earnest petition for a fuller knowledge of these blessings.

Read Ephesians 1:15-23

1. What prompts Paul to launch into prayer for his readers?

2. Paul applauds their *faith in the Lord Jesus* and *love for all the saints*. Why is this combination so obviously basic to being a Christian?

3. Whom does Paul see as the author of both qualities?

4. Although Paul is thankful for these believers in Ephesus, what is his basic request for them (verse 17)?

5. What is Paul talking about when he speaks of *the eyes of your heart* in verse 18?

6. Into what three areas of knowledge does Paul want his readers to have wisdom and insight (verses 18, 19)?

   Why is insight from God necessary for the kind of understanding Paul is praying for?

7. What is *the hope* (verse 18) to which God calls us?

   Compare with what Paul writes in Romans 8:18-25.

8. What kind of an inheritance does God have for us in Christ (verse 18; 1 Peter 1:3-5; Romans 8:15-17).

   How does this encourage you as a Christian believer?

9. What is the scope of the power available to you in Christ (verses 19-21)?

   How can a growing understanding of that power affect your own life in times of difficulty?

10. How are the past, present and future of your walk of faith covered by God's call, your inheritance and God's available power?

11. What position and authority does Christ have right now (verses 19-23)?

    How does this compare with your ideas of his power?

12. What do you learn about the relationship between Christ and the Father?

13. How is the word ***church*** defined in verses 22 and 23?

    How is this different from the local church down the street?

14. What type of union or interdependence exists between the human head and the human body?

    What truth does Paul point out by his use of ***head*** in verse 22 and the ***body*** in verse 23?

15. What new possibilities do you see for yourself or your group if you pray verses 17-19 into your lives?

Summary

1. What impresses you most about the description of God in this prayer?

   About the Spirit's work?

   About Christ's work?

2. What is one change you need to make if you give Christ his rightful place as ***head***?

Prayer

God of our Lord Jesus Christ, glorious Father, we come to you in Jesus' name. We don't know you nearly as well as we want to, and so we make Paul's prayer our own. In your grace, please enlighten our hearts so that we will see and desire all that you have for us. Help us to give Christ his rightful place in our lives that we may indeed live to the praise of your glory. Amen.

DISCUSSION 4

Alive in Christ

Ephesians 2:1-10

The Christian gospel is first bad news and then good news. Over the centuries human beings have found it hard to come to terms with the bad news because it insists that we cannot make ourselves good enough for God. This hurts our pride. These ten verses from Paul's letter give a realistic picture of human beings, but also are full of optimism about God's grace. This section is a continuation of Paul's prayer that we would come to know God's *incomparably great power for us who believe* (1:18, 19). God raised Christ from the dead; he can also raise us spiritually from the dead.

As a part of your preparation for this discussion, list in two columns the condition of people before (verses 1-3) and after (verses 4-10) salvation by Christ.

Read Ephesians 2:1-10

1. Who is the *you* Paul addresses in this section?

2. Speaking of *you* Gentiles and *us/we* Jews, how does Paul describe the universal human condition?

3. Read verses 1-3 in NIV, NEB, GNB. In what sense are unredeemed people *dead*?

How can people be dead even while they are living? Compare with 4:18.

4. What loyalties do such people have?

   What actions characterize them?

   In their natural condition, what is their destiny (verse 3)?

*Note: **Transgressions** (verse 1), straying from the right road; **sins**, failure to be what we ought to be and could be; **wrath** (verse 3), God's personal, righteous, constant hostility toward evil.*

5. What amazing change has taken place in the people to whom Paul writes?

6. Why and how did God accomplish this?

7. In verses 5-8 what is referred to as past?

   As future?

   As present?

8. Why can't we work our way into God's favor (verses 1, 3, 8-10)?

9. In contrast to what Paul says in verses 1-10, what does trying to work for our salvation imply about God and about ourselves?

10. What place do good works have in your life *after* you have been **made alive with Christ, saved** (verse 10)?

11. How does verse 10 relate to being *to the praise of his glorious grace* in 1:6?

Summary

1. What does Paul want his readers to know about God and about their relationship to him through Jesus Christ?

2. Into what two classifications does Paul divide all people?

   How can a person move from one classification to the other?

3. What changes should take place in the person who becomes a Christian?

Prayer

Lord God, in spite of all you offer us, many people are still trying to work their way to heaven. Maybe some of us are among them. We begin to trust you, but then we think the good news is too good to be true. Help us to understand the gospel so thoroughly that we accept you by faith and live by faith, daily trusting your great mercy and grace towards us. We bring our spiritual poverty to you that you may fill our lives with your richness. For the praise of your glory. Amen.

Ephesians

DISCUSSION 5

God's New Society

Ephesians 2:11-22

Alienation is not only a contemporary word but a common experience for many in our society. People are separated from one another by color, economics, education, and ideas. Sometimes alienation becomes hatred. Walls are erected, barriers that cannot be crossed. These may even appear in a church.

The study for today deals primarily with the division between Jew and Gentile. Jews had so many advantages over the Gentiles. They were God's people; the truth about God had been given to them. The first Christians were Jewish. Jews had no dealings with Gentiles, but then Gentiles heard the message about Jesus and also believed. How could the Christian church include both Jews and Gentiles?

Read Ephesians 2:11-13

1. How desperate was the situation of the Gentiles before Christ came (verses 12, 13)?

2. In contrast, what advantages did the Jews have?

Note: Circumcision was the sign of God's covenant with Israel, the seal that they were God's people (Genesis 17:7-

14). In the most private areas of their lives, Jews were to be reminded that they belonged to the Lord. But the physical must also be a matter of the heart. God wanted circumcised hearts.

3. Why are physical marks or any other religious rite unable to make a person right with God (2:3-5)?

   What needs to be taken care of?

4. Note the progression of thought in verse 12: *separate from Christ... excluded from citizenship... foreigners... without hope... without God.* What does it mean to you to say that someone is *without God?*

5. What difference does the coming of Christ make for the *separate... excluded... foreigners... without hope and without God* today (verse 13)?

6. How could you use verse 13 as a definition of what it means to become a Christian?

Read Ephesians 2:14-18

7. Before Christ came, Jew and Gentile were separated by a mutual animosity and contempt, by an actual wall between Jewish and Gentile areas in the temple, and by God's commandments given only to the Jews. But Paul repeatedly uses the words *peace* and *one* to describe the new relationship between Jews and Gentiles in Christ. How did Christ break down the barriers and bring peace between Jew and Gentile?

8. What is Christ's goal in doing this (verses 15b, 16, 18)?

9. How do both Jew and Gentile now come to God?

10. As a Christian, what do you have in common with other Christian believers of divergent backgrounds—whatever their race, nationality or denomination?

    What walls have you felt broken down because of your faith in Christ?

Read Ephesians 2:19-22

11. What are the consequences of Christ's death for *all* Christians?

12. How do the pictures of a new citizenship, a family and a building, help you understand what Christ's death made possible for all Christians?

    What does each example tell you about privileges, loyalties, responsibilities?

13. Paul compares Christian believers to a temple being constructed. Upon what does the unity and the stability of this whole new building depend (verses 20, 21)?

14. What is the purpose of the temple Christ is building (verses 21, 22)?

    How do you know the temple is not finished yet?

15. How can you cooperate with or resist God in building you into this temple for his dwelling place?

Summary

1. What did it cost Christ to bring about unity, to create one new humanity?

2. In view of this cost, what can you do to strengthen your ties with other Christian believers?

3. What privilege is yours which surpasses even that of fellowship with other Christians (verses 18, 22)?

Note: God's exclusiveness consists in planning everything in and through Jesus Christ. Man's exclusiveness consists in choosing secondary factors and making them primary.

Prayer

*Lord Jesus Christ, thank you for being our peace, for breaking down the dividing wall that kept us from God and from other believers. We are thankful to be included in what you are building—your church around the world. We are humbled to be part of a temple where God lives by his Spirit. Help us to share in making peace by telling the good news of your salvation to people who are alienated, who are without God and without hope. We praise you for letting us be known by your name—the **Christians**. For the praise of your glory. Amen.*

DISCUSSION 6

Sent to the Gentiles

Ephesians 3:1-13

Paul was given a unique role when he was converted. Acts 9 tells how Paul (then known as Saul) was on his way to the synagogues of Damascus to arrest any who believed in Jesus. Blinded by a dazzling light, Paul fell to the ground when the risen Lord Jesus spoke to him. The Lord gave Paul three days to think over what had happened before he sent a disciple named Ananias to restore his sight, saying, *"This man is my chosen instrument to carry my name before the Gentiles and their kings and before the people of Israel. I will show him how much he must suffer for my name"* (Acts 9:15).

Later on Paul's missionary journeys, he went first to the Jewish synagogues to tell them about Jesus, but he did not limit the message of salvation to Jews only. Paul's preaching to the Gentiles and including them in the church of Christ stirred up opposition and led to his arrest.

Read Ephesians 3:1-6

1. As he wrote this letter, Paul was a prisoner in Rome awaiting trial before Nero. What does the way he describes his situation in verse 1 indicate about his view of life?

2. When you have negative circumstances, how do you evaluate your situation?

   In what ways does your point of view change your circumstances?

3. The phrase *for this reason* refers to the previous paragraphs. Put in your own words a summary of what Paul has been saying about the Gentiles.

4. Paul interrupts himself in verse 2. As he elaborates on the responsibility God has given him, Paul uses the word *mystery* three times. What is the mystery to which he refers (verses 3-6; 1:9, 10)?

Note: Paul moves from a general statement in 1:9, 10, to specific details in 3:6.

5. How did Paul come to understand this mystery? Compare verse 3 and Acts 9:1-6, 10-19.

6. Put into your own words the three statements Paul makes about the Gentile Christians in 3:6.

   How does this contrast with their former condition in 2:12?

7. What brought about this dramatic change for these people?

Read Ephesians 3:7-13

8. In what sense could Paul say that becoming *a servant of this gospel* is a *gift* (verse 7)?

   In what ways is he awed by this gift?

9. How does Paul describe the privilege of spreading the gospel (verses 8, 9)?

10. Read verse 8 in several contemporary versions. From your own experience, what are *the unsearchable riches of Christ* that Paul speaks about?

    How did you come to understand whatever you know about these riches?

11. For what purpose has God let you have some understanding of the riches of Christ?

12. This new society, the group of those who have been reconciled to God, Paul calls *the church* (verse 10). What is the purpose of the church in God's plan (verses 6, 10, 11)?

    How do these verses change your understanding of what the church is?

13. How was God's eternal plan accomplished (verses 10, 11)?

14. What amazing privilege does this give to every Christian (verse 12)?

    What difference does this make in your praying and worship?

Summary

1. From what you have studied thus far in Ephesians, what have you learned about *the church* and how it is central in God's plan?

What can you do to share the gospel with people of diverse cultural and racial backgrounds and to help your church welcome them?

2. In spite of all his privileges and responsibilities, Paul has a humble view of himself. What effect does humility in Christian leaders have upon their work for Christ and their attitude toward those they serve?

Prayer

Thank you, Lord God, for revealing the mystery of your will to your servant Paul so that we might hear the gospel of Jesus Christ. Help us to be faithful links in the chain of those who communicate your message to the ends of the earth. We praise you that this Good News is for every person who will respond to the gift of your grace. What a privilege it is to be part of the church, the body of those who have been redeemed by the death of Christ. We look forward to the day when some from every tribe and nation will be gathered at your throne to the praise of your glorious grace. Amen.

DISCUSSION 7

For This Reason I Kneel

Ephesians 3:14-21

We pray about *what* concerns us. Analyzing what we pray for reveals much about the quality of our Christian lives. This is Paul's second prayer in this letter. That alone tells us something about Paul. Paul has been explaining God's peace—the reconciling work of Christ Jesus that gave birth to the church—God's new society. He has shared the awe he feels over his personal involvement in this. From Paul's overflowing heart we now hear him pray for believers.

Read Ephesians 3:14-21

1. What does Paul's position as he prays tell you about the intensity of his concern?

Note: The normal posture for prayer among the Jews was standing with outstretched hands, palms upward. Kneeling was unusual.

2. Paul picks up his thought from verse 1 of this chapter. What moves him to pray (2:19-22; 3:6)?

3. What effect should the knowledge of God's purpose have on your prayers?

4. What do you learn about God from the way Paul addresses him (verses 14-16; 1:2, 3, 17; 2:18, 22)?

   The fatherhood of God gives Paul confidence in praying for these Gentile believers. What confidence does it give to you in your praying?

5. Why would Paul want them to know that he is praying to the God who has *glorious riches* (verse 16)?

   What difference does that knowledge make to you?

6. What basic gifts does Paul ask for in his petitions (verses 16-19)?

   How would these gifts meet your inner needs?

*Note: The Greeks used the phrase **the inner man** to include a person's reason, conscience and will. The **heart** included not only a person's affections but the intelligence and will also.*

7. For what purpose does Paul want believers strengthened (verses 18, 19)?

8. How do God's power, knowledge, and fullness come to you?

9. How does Paul emphasize the vastness of the love of Christ (verses 17-19)?

   In whose company do we come to understand something of the love of Christ (verse 18)?

   What does that tell you about the folly of trying to be a "lone ranger" Christian?

10. Why is there always more to know of Christ's love?

11. According to 3:19 and 2:22, what should be the goal of every Christian and of the church?

*Note: The **fullness of God** includes all of God's excellencies and perfection. It is the moral qualities of God embodied in Jesus Christ which Christians understand increasingly as Christ dwells in their hearts by faith.*

12. What impresses you about Paul's requests in verses 16-19?

13. Of what truth about God does Paul remind us in his closing benediction (verse 20)?

14. How does God receive glory in the church?

    In Christ Jesus?

    For how long?

Summary

1. Think about the words you would use to describe God to a friend or a child. What words or phrases from Paul's prayer would help you?

2. How do you want to be prayed for as a result of this study?

Prayer

Each of you choose one of Paul's requests and pray it for the person sitting next to you. Use that person's name, and simply ask God as our Father, out of his glorious riches, to give _____ this gift (name the gift from Paul's prayer), for Jesus' sake.

Discussion 8

We Belong to One Another

Ephesians 4:1-16

Paul has spelled out some immense concepts for the believers reading this letter. He has shared the mind-stretching revelation God has given him that all things are to be united in Christ Jesus. The church, the body of Christ, is to be Christ's instrument to make this message known. But Paul is also practical. Now, he says, *this* is how it works out in real life. The last half of his letter gives standards for the church, the new society God has created.

Read Ephesians 4:1-6

1. By saying *therefore* or *then*, Paul refers his reader's back to his previous reasoning. What is the *calling* believers have received?

   Compare 1:4-6, 11, 12; 2:10, 13, 19-22; 3:10.

2. Give a synonym for each of the four virtues Paul uses in verse 2 to describe a life worthy of the name Christian.

3. How do these virtues affect Paul's instruction in verse 3?

4. How do you know that this unity is not man-made (verses 4-6)?

Note: Paul emphasizes the maintenance or the keeping of the unity of the Spirit. Christians are not able to create or organize this kind of unity.

5. What are seven distinguishing features of the unity which exists among Christians?

   What part do the Father, Son and Holy Spirit play in this Christian unity?

6. From this description of its unity, how would you define what the *church* is?

7. What truth does Paul bring out about unity by referring here to God as the *Father* of all believers rather than as the King or the Judge?

Note: The true church is invisible, its members known only to God. This church can never be split. However, the visible church is made up of individual congregations. In fact, this letter addressed to the Ephesians is probably a circular letter sent to several churches in Asia Minor. Paul is urging these Christians to maintain unity in the visible church. We are to show to the world that the unity that exists indestructibly in the Spirit is a genuine thing in actual practice in local congregations and between congregations.

Read Ephesians 4:7-13

8. What diversity exists alongside of the unity just described?

   Who is the source of the talents and abilities given to individual Christians (verses 7, 8)?

Note: His mention of the ascended Christ leads Paul into a parenthetical statement about him in verses 9, 10.

9. What gifts are given to Christ's body, the church, and for what purpose (verses 11-13)?

10. Rather than promoting pride, how does remembering that you are God-gifted help you develop the humility, gentleness, patience and love commanded in verse 2?

11. What is the difference between the ***unity of the Spirit*** (verse 3) and ***unity in the faith and in the knowledge of the Son of God*** (verse 13)?

    How can you guard the first and make the second a reality in your life?

12. How would you describe the ultimate goal of Christian maturity from 4:13 and 3:19?

Read Ephesians 4:14-16

13. How does Paul illustrate spiritual immaturity (verse 14)?

    How can you avoid being an unstable Christian?

14. How does Paul describe genuine Christian maturity (verses 15, 16)?

15. Give an example of a way you can ***speak the truth in love*** (verse 15)?

    How is this different from ***cunning and craftiness*** and ***deceitful scheming*** (verse 14)?

16. Why do you need the other members of the body of Christ (verses 11-13, 15, 16)?

Summary

1. How does Paul's description of the church affect your vision for your church?

2. How can you participate in the work of your church to help bring everyone to spiritual maturity?

Prayer

Father God, thank you that your Spirit gives unity to the church that Jesus Christ died to save. We are aware of our calling by your grace. We want to live the kind of life that is worthy of the name Christian. Thank you for placing us in a body of people whom you have gifted to teach us and help us to grow to maturity in our faith. We pray that you will help us to be and to act like grown-up Christians. For the praise of your glory. Amen.

DISCUSSION 9

New Clothes to Wear

Ephesians 4:17-32

You need new clothes if you are going to live a new life. No more living as though you were a pagan, Paul says. The believers had become different people; they were to live a different kind of life. Paul wants his readers to understand the contrast. His instructions in this study are both specific and practical. They also are given with apostolic authority: *I tell you this, and insist on it in the Lord* (4:17).

Read Ephesians 4:17-24

1. What is Paul's major concern about these new Christians living in the pagan Gentile culture (verses 17-19)?

2. For the Gentiles outside of Christ, what is wrong with their thinking?

3. What downward spiral develops in their thoughts and actions?

    Compare with Romans 1:21-25.

Ephesians

4. What is the obvious connection between the way a person thinks, what he puts into his mind, and the way he acts?

   How does a person harden his heart?

5. In contrast to the ignorance, futility and darkness of pagan minds, what words give an opposite picture of the minds of believers (verses 20, 22-24)?

6. What three things must Christian believers do in preparation for a new lifestyle (verses 22-24)?

7. In order to obey the instruction to *put off your old self* and *put on the new self*, what practical actions must you take?

8. How can you *be made new in the attitude of your minds*?

   Compare verses 23, 24 and Romans 8:5.

9. What impresses you about the goal God has for every Christian (verse 24)?

Read Ephesians 4:25-32

10. Paul gives a series of concrete examples of what to put off and what to put on. In each case what are we to get rid of and what is to replace it?

11. What reasons are given for each of these changes of conduct?

    Which of these reasons surprises you?

12. How would each of these instructions about behavior affect relationships and the unity of the body of Christ?

13. What do you learn here about the right way to handle anger (verses 26, 27, 31)?

    What dangers accompany anger?

14. What kinds of behavior grieve the Holy Spirit?

15. What do the attitudes of verse 31 have in common?

    Why are they so destructive?

16. In contrast, what standard does Paul set in verse 32?

    Why should we act in this way toward others?

Summary

1. Paul describes the non-Christian society of his day. What insights does it give you into the non-Christian society of our day?

   What same effects of sin are evident today in the mind and heart and body?

2. What do you learn about the importance of your daily choices from this study?

Prayer

Father God, make our new life as obvious to others as new clothes. Remind us of even the smallest places in our lives where we need to abandon old ways and put on new ways of thinking and acting. Help us to treat one another as Jesus Christ has treated us. Teach us by your Spirit; help us to learn from your word; fill us with the love of Jesus Christ. For the praise of your glory. Amen.

DISCUSSION 10

Light and Darkness

Ephesians 5:1-20

When Paul urges us to wear appropriate clothing that matches our commitment to Christ, he is not talking about superficial trimmings on the outside. Believers, redeemed at great cost, have been given a new life. A radical change in lifestyle comes from a changed heart. Remember that Paul's letter did not have the chapter divisions we have in our texts. This study is a continuation of his arguments for right thinking and right living begun in the last part of chapter four. Now he concentrates on our motivation for holy living. He begins by telling us who our model is. *As children copy their fathers, you, as God's children, are to copy Him* (Phillips' translation).

*As part of your study of verses 1-20 for this discussion, make two columns, titled **darkness** and **light**. List in the appropriate column the thoughts, words and actions which characterize the old life and the new life.*

Read Ephesians 5:1-20

1. In what particular area should Christians imitate God, and why (verses 1, 2)?

Ephesians

What example does Paul give to help us understand the quality of love he is talking about?

2. What behaviors are improper for God's holy people (verses 3-7)?

   Contrast the self-sacrifice of verse 2 with the self-indulgence of verse 3.

3. Why is greed linked with sexual immorality and impurity (verse 3)?

   Why would a greedy (covetous) person be called an idol worshiper (verse 5)?

4. How is the kind of language named in verse 4 incompatible with thankfulness?

   What harm is there in the coarse talk and vulgarities so common in today's world?

5. State four reasons Paul gives for why Christians should abstain from an immoral lifestyle (verses 3-7).

   What would continuation in such a lifestyle indicate about one's basic beliefs?

6. Paul says, **Let no one deceive you.** How are people today being deceived in the area of sexual sin?

7. Give examples of how Christians today face the choices in verses 7-11.

8. Paul says Christians are **light in the Lord, children of light**. What does light produce (verse 9), and in doing this what does it reveal (verses 11, 13, 14)?

Why would anyone prefer darkness to light?

Note: The New English Bible reads, ***Live like people who are at home in the daylight.*** *Verse 14 is probably a quotation from an early Christian hymn, perhaps a baptismal hymn, a summons to a new life.*

9. What gives Paul a sense of urgency in his warnings in verses 15-17?

10. From your study of this letter, what practical decisions have you made to live in our society as a *wise* Christian (verse 15)?

11. What two patterns of social life are contrasted in verse 18?

12. What does it mean to be *filled with the Spirit*?

    In contrast to the debauchery from being drunk on wine, what practices, attitudes and relationships result from being filled with the Holy Spirit?

13. What do the phrases *to one another* and *to the Lord* add to your understanding of this Spirit-filled lifestyle (verses 17-20)?

Summary

1. Observe all the major contrasts you find in this section of Ephesians (i.e. light/darkness, wise/foolish, etc.).

   Why would anyone ever choose to live in the negatives of the list you have just made?

2. What characterizes the life of the person who chooses to live as a child of light?

Think of one area of your life that needs to be exposed more to the light of Christ's love. Make this need your daily prayer this week.

Prayer

Our Heavenly Father, we want to live as children of light. Help us to submit our wills to your will, so that we make the moral choices that reveal we are your children. We want to be like you. Thank you for the gift of the Holy Spirit who teaches us and guides us into truth. Help us to get rid of whatever keeps him from filling our lives. Give us a life that shares your goodness in love with others, that sings to you, and that is full of thanksgiving. For the praise of your glory. Amen.

DISCUSSION 11

New Relationships

Ephesians 5:21—6:9

Paul's teaching about a new lifestyle had centered on unity and purity. In this study he addresses the relationships which are basic to human existence: husbands and wives, parents and children, masters and servants. Far from being repressive in his teaching, Paul's instructions elevate the standards for relationships beyond anything known in the ancient world. The dominant male had absolute power over women and children, and masters owned their slaves. God is building a new society, Paul says. It demands mutual submission; all persons are equal before God, whatever their societal role.

Read Ephesians 5:21—6:9

1. How does verse 21 serve both as a suitable conclusion to the previous paragraph (verses 15-20) and a comprehensive introduction to our present study?

2. What does it mean to *submit* to another?

   What word would you use to express the opposite meaning?

3. Who is to submit to whom in verse 21? Why?

4. In what way is submission the responsibility of every person in the relationships addressed in this study?

5. Why do people resist the concept of submission?

6. What was Christ's motive and what were his purposes in his sacrificial death for the church (verses 25-28)?

   How are these the key to understanding Paul's comparison between marriage and the relationship between Christ and the church?

7. What is the reason for Christ's continuing care for the church (verses 29, 30)?

8. What is the church's response to Christ (verse 24)?

9. Comparing the responsibilities of a wife to her husband with those of a husband to his wife, which are the more demanding?

10. How does the example of Christ's goal for the church instruct a husband and protect a wife from tyranny?

    Instead of urging the exercise of authority, what are Paul's instructions to husbands?

11. What would it mean today for a husband to love his wife as he loves himself?

12. How would the responsibilities of a wife to her husband work out in everyday living today (verses 22-24, 33)?

13. How does Paul's teaching about husbands and wives and Christ and the church, elevate the quality and stability of marriage (verses 28-32)?

14. Why should children be taught to obey both their father and their mother (6:1-3)?

    What does *in the Lord* mean?

    What does it mean to *honor* your father and mother?

15. What warning and what positive instruction are addressed particularly to fathers? Compare Colossians 3:21.

16. Although Paul wrote in the context of widespread slavery, how does the teaching of 6:5-9 apply to employer-employee relationships?

17. What kind of integrity do you see that this demands of you as an employee or employer in the workplace (6:5-9)?

18. In what way does Paul's instruction to masters essentially break the power of slavery (6:9)? Compare Colossians 4:1.

Summary

1. What does Paul expect to see as evidence of Christ's rule in personal relationships between Christians?

2. Describe the kind of society that obedience to the teaching of this study would bring about.

3. Which of these instructions do you need to work on?

Prayer

Father God, thank you that love and responsibility go together in your sight. Thank you for the way you take responsibility for us, both in loving us and in helping us to become what you want us to be. Thank you that you keep your promises. Help us to keep ours. Teach us new things about living together in your sight as members of your family. In a world that emphasizes rights, may we honor one another as made in the image of God, and readily respond to the responsibilities you have given us. Help us to keep in mind the sacrifice of the cross, to follow your example of humility and service for others. For the praise of your glory. Amen.

DISCUSSION 12

Stand Firm

Ephesians 6:10-24

Paul began this letter by unfolding God's purposes from the very beginning. God's plan was to create one new people in Christ Jesus, a people who would belong to him, who would inherit all he has for them. Sometimes Paul seems to strain for words glorious enough to tell all he knows about God's plan. He discusses the practical matters of unity, diversity, purity and harmony in this new family of God, and instructs us that *new life equals new lifestyle*. But now Paul is near the end of his letter and he faces the realities of spiritual conflict. He reminds us that we have an enemy. Opposition will come from the devil who doesn't want to see any of this put in place. Paul tells us how to respond when under attack.

Read Ephesians 6:10-20

1. When opposition comes it is easy to say, "I knew it was too good to be true!" How do you know that is not the case here?

2. What do the commands to be strong, put on full armor and take your stand indicate about this conflict, and your resources?

3. Why do you need *the armor of God* (verses 11, 13; 1 Peter 5:8, 9)?

4. What is the nature and area of operation of the Christian's enemies (verses 11-16)?

   Why is it impossible to fight the devil's strategies (verses 11 and 16) with your own resources?

5. Which equipment is for defense, and which for offense?

6. In what ways do the belt and the breastplate protect the believer?

   Give a practical example from your own life.

Note: ***Truth...righteousness*** *(verse 14)—Quality of character, moral integrity and righteous living, as in 4:24-32; 5:8-11; Isaiah 11:5; 59:17.*

7. Every soldier knows the value of good shoes. How does this part of the armor help you to stand firm?

Note: ***Let the shoes on your feet be the gospel of peace, to give you firm footing*** *(verse 15, NEB)—Really understanding the gospel of peace (2:14-18) keeps the Christian, described as a frontline soldier, from slipping and falling back when the enemy charges.*

8. How is *faith* the Christian's chief means of protection?

Note: ***Shield*** *(verse 16), the Roman soldier's large oblong shield of wood and water-soaked leather, fitted together with others, made a wall before and a roof overhead to absorb and quench the enemy's flaming arrows.*

In what form might the devil's flaming arrows come today?

Note: James 1:14; 1 Peter 2:11; Ephesians 4:22, 25-31.

9. Why does the head need special protection?

   What attacks might come through your mind?

10. How would the sure knowledge of our salvation (2:5-8) protect us from attacks through our mind?

    Give an example from your own life.

11. How can your one offensive weapon be used?

    Whose sword is it?

12. It's important for a soldier to keep in contact with headquarters and other soldiers. How does this relate to verse 18?

13. What are Paul's special prayer requests for the battle he is in (verses 19, 20)?

    What does the repetition of *fearlessly* reveal about Paul?

Read Ephesians 6:21-24

14. How is Tychicus suited for the job Paul is giving him?

15. In what way are *peace, love, faith,* and *grace* in Paul's closing benediction a fitting conclusion for this letter?

Summary of the Letter to the Ephesians

1. What life-changing truths have you learned about God's purposes in human history that affect your life?

2. What does it mean to you to be *in Christ*?

3. How should a Christian live in society to let the truth about Christ be known to an unbelieving world?

Prayer

Praise be to you, the God and Father of our Lord Jesus Christ, who has blessed us with every spiritual blessing. Thank you for saving us by your grace, and teaching us how rich and strong your promises are. You have equipped us with all we need to lead a godly life in the kind of world in which we live. We are thankful for spiritual armor that you designed to fit our needs. Now, Lord God, we thank you for all we have learned from this letter. Write its truths on our hearts and minds, and help us to live out what we have come to understand. For the praise of your glory. Amen.

What Should Our Group Study Next?

New Groups and Outreach Groups
How To Start A Neighborhood Bible Study
Mark *(recommended as first unit of study)*
Acts
John, Book 1 *(Chapters 1-10)*
John, Book 2 *(Chapters 11-21)*
Four Men of God *(Abraham, Joseph, Moses, David)*
Romans
1 John and James
Genesis *(Chapters 1-25)*

Groups Reaching People from Non-Christian Cultures
Genesis *(Chapters 1-25)*
Mark
Four Men of God *(Abraham, Joseph, Moses, David)*
Romans
1 Corinthians
Lifestyles of Faith

Advanced Groups/ Sunday School (Adult and Older Teens)
Matthew, Book 1 *(Chapters 1-16)*
Matthew, Book 2 *(Chapters 17-28)*
Courage to Cope
Four Men of God *(Abraham, Joseph, Moses, David)*
1 & 2 Peter *(Letters to People in Trouble)*
Hebrews
The Coming of the Lord
(1 & 2 Thessalonians, 2 & 3 John, Jude)
Prophets of Hope *(Haggai, Zechariah, Malachi)*
Promises from God
2 Corinthians
Galatians & Philemon
Isaiah
Servants of the Lord
Work - God's Gift
Lifestyles of Faith

Biweekly or Monthly Groups
They Met Jesus *(8 Studies of N.T. Characters)*
Celebrate
Courage to Cope
Psalms & Proverbs
Servants of the Lord
Work - God's Gift
Lifestyles of Faith

ALL studies in this series available from:

Neighborhood Bible Studies
34 Main Street
Dobbs Ferry, New York 10522
1-800-369-0307

About Neighborhood Bible Studies

Neighborhood Bible Studies, Inc. (NBS) is a leader in the field of small group discussion Bible studies. Since 1960, NBS has pioneered the development of Bible study groups that encourage each member to participate in the leadership of the discussion.

The **ministry** of Neighborhood Bible Studies provides people with the opportunity to discover the truths of Scripture for themselves. Through these small group discussion Bible studies, men and women:

- encounter Jesus Christ
- choose to obey him
- mature in faith.

NBS **methods** and **materials** are used around the world to:

- equip individuals for facilitating discovery Bible studies
- serve as a resource to the church.

Skilled NBS personnel conduct workshops and seminars to train individuals, clergy and laity in how to establish small group Bible studies in neighborhoods, churches, workplaces and specialized facilities. Publication in more than 25 languages indicates the use of NBS cross-culturally.

Churches from a wide range of denominations use the NBS materials and methods to:

- develop a program of outreach Bible studies
- give electives for high school and adult classes
- build support groups within the church fellowship to encourage spiritual nourishment.

About the Authors

Marilyn Kunz and **Catherine Schell**, authors of the NBS series of discussion guides, founded Neighborhood Bible Studies and directed its work for thirty-one years.

COMPLETE LISTING of NBS STUDY GUIDES

Getting Started
How To Start A Neighborhood Bible Study *handbook & video*

Bible Book Studies
Genesis, Chapters 1-25 *Beginnings with God*
Psalms & Proverbs *Perspective and Wisdom for Today*
Isaiah *God's Help Is on the Way*
Haggai, Zechariah, and Malachi *Prophets of Hope*
Matthew, Book One *God's Promise Fulfilled*
Matthew, Book Two *God's Purpose Fulfilled*
Mark *Hope for Hurting People*
Luke *Good News and Great Joy*
John, Book One *Believe and See*
John, Book Two *Believe and Live*
Acts, Book One *A New Beginning*
Acts, Book Two *Paul Sets the Pattern*
Romans *A Reasoned Faith...A Reasonable Faith*
1 Corinthians *Finding Answers to Life's Questions*
2 Corinthians *The Power of Weakness*
Galatians & Philemon *Fully Accepted By God*
Ephesians *Living in God's Family*
Philippians *A Message of Encouragement*
Colossians *Staying Focused on Truth*
1 & 2 Thessalonians, 2 & 3 John, Jude *The Coming of the Lord*
Hebrews *Unveiling Jesus Christ*
1 & 2 Peter *Letters to People in Trouble*
1 John & James *Faith that Knows and Shows*

Topical Studies
Celebrate *Reasons for Hurrahs*
Coping with Stress *Insights from Eight Bible Leaders*
Courage to Cope *Uncommon Resources*
Lenten Studies *Life Defeats Death*
Promises from God *Hope that Doesn't Disappoint*
Servants of the Lord *Living by God's Agenda*
Set Free *Leaving Negative Emotions Behind*
Work - God's Gift *Life-Changing Choices*

Character Studies
Four Men of God *Unlikely Leaders*
Lifestyles of Faith, Book One *Choosing to Trust God*
Lifestyles of Faith, Book Two *Choosing to Obey God*
They Met Jesus *Life-Changing Encounters*